Dedicated to Kitty

CAT

I woke up this morning purring...
There was a cat inside of me.
"What are you doing in there?" I asked.
"You're not meant to be inside of me!"

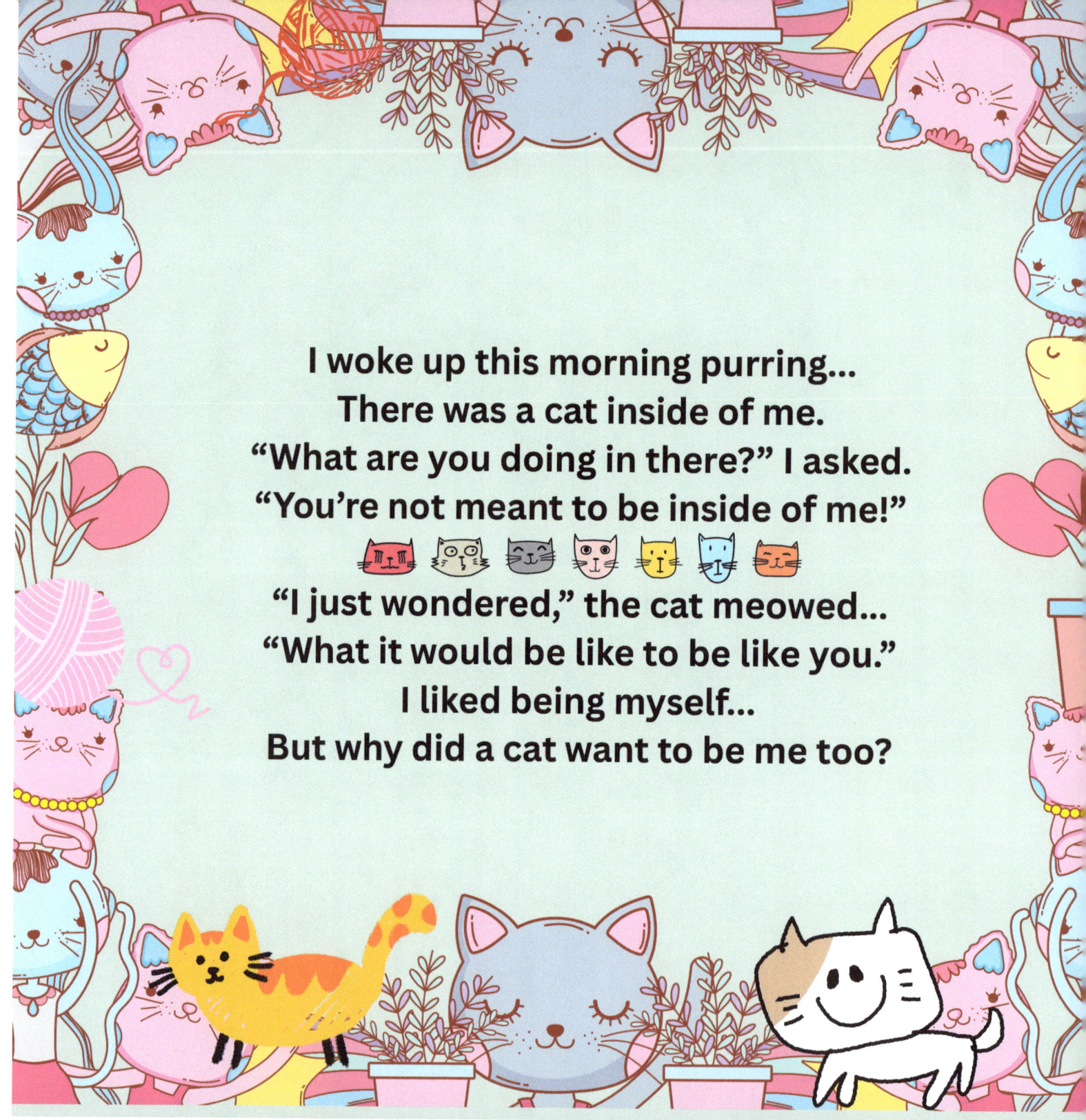

"I just wondered," the cat meowed...
"What it would be like to be like you."
I liked being myself...
But why did a cat want to be me too?

"You can talk!" the cat explained.
"And you can meow!" I replied.
"You can flush the toilet!" the cat said.
Which was one truth I couldn't deny.

"And you live with your family," she said.
"While I don't even remember mine!"
"But you are a member of our family!"
I said.
"You're my sister feline!"

The next thing I knew the cat jumped out...
She was no longer inside of me.
I guess she decided she loved being my cat...
As much as I love being me!

GRACKLE

"I'd never heard of a grackle before...
Until one flew inside of me.
She said she was a member of
The blackbird family.

"Why me?" I asked.
Since no one had chosen me before.
Once she was inside my tummy
She made sounds like a squeaky door.

"Now I think I understand why you chose me!"
I said.
She listened patiently...
"Was it because neither of us fit in," I asked
"With how others think we ought to be?"

I'm not sure if she knew what I meant...
But she and I seemed to agree...
We could sing together in a duet
Since both of our voices were squeaky!

CRICKET

Cricket TV

Grandma told me the crickets called to her!
Then one moved inside of me.
Now when we sit together on the sofa...
We listen to the cricket symphony.

Grandma said crickets always followed her...
Even when she was a little girl like me.
She says she and I are kindred spirits...
They love her, so they also love me.

Grandma takes my hand into hers...
The crickets invite us to join their symphony.
Grandma and I think about it...
But decide they already play perfectly.

EXIT

MAZE

If you've ever been lost in a maze...
Like me you probably felt forlorn.
That is exactly how I felt...
When I got lost in a maze of corn!

I found my way out...
Eventually...
I ran home and discovered
A maze inside of me!

Now I practice every day...
Finding my own way out...
Planning and keeping track...
Without feeling the need to shout!

What I learned by having...
A maze inside of me...
Is I can always find my own way out...
Leaving a trail of maize (corn kernels) is key!

PRAYING MANTIS

I saw a praying mantis
The praying mantis saw me.
We stared into each other's eyes...
Then he flew inside of me.

He taught me how to pray
I taught him how to play
Great friends we came to be
The praying mantis and me!

BEETLE

I had a ride in a car called a beetle...
I admit the ride was a little bumpy.
When the engine slowed it down...
A beetle flew inside of me.

I prefer the bug to the car...
It is quiet and doesn't bother me.
I hope the car hits the road soon...
It BEEP BEEPS ANNOYINGLY!

Every life contains a secret
And there's one inside of me!
It whispers and it whispers
In secrecy.

Mommy and Daddy think..
I'm listening quietly...
They are right I am listening...
And hoping the secret soon reveals itself to me.

Shhh...

"What is my secret?" I ask.
"That's for me to know," the secret says...
"And for you to find out!"
Then she whispers and whispers for days!

I love secrets...
Especially when they live inside of me.
But I can't wait until the day
My secret is no longer a secret TO ME!

TRIFLE

A trifle means a wee thing...
But it's not the kind of trifle inside of me!
This trifle is a kind of dessert...
Made of custard, fruit and jelly!

MULE

They tell me mules can be stubborn...
Now there's one inside of me.
He refuses to do any kind of work...
All he does is EEE-AWW at me!

"Sit!" I command.
My dog follows what I say.
But the mule sure doesn't...
And he ignores me by the way!

A mule is super stubborn!
Especially this one inside of me!
He won't even follow...
When I invite him to dinner with the family!

Daddy says I shouldn't worry.
The mule will eat when he gets hungry.
But I wonder how he will find food...
When he's stuck inside of me!

MAGPIE

I didn't know Canada had magpies...
Until one flew inside of me.
He is a black billed magpie...
And he is a real beauty!

He told me he needed refuge...
From the Canadian wintery weather...
Since we both had that in common...
We decided to stick together!

MOONLIGHT

The moonlight in the daytime...
Lives inside of me.
I often wonder if...
Without it the stars get lonely.

MEGRIM

I woke up with something called a
MEGRIM inside of me.
I didn't know what a MEGRIM WAS...
Nor what it might do to me!

I asked it - it didn't answer...
But my head hurt me.
Is this I wondered...
What a MEGRIM is meant to be?

Mom suggested I eat breakfast...
Dad said a glass of water was the cure...
I tried both of their suggestions...
I wanted to be MEGRIM sure!

And soon that old MEGRIM
Went as quickly as it came.
A MEGRIM is a kind of headache...
I hope it never comes back again!

LINT

The other day I found some lint...
Inside the button in my belly...
And now a giant lint ball
Lives inside of me!

It's so big!
Bigger than a basketball!
It makes my tummy feel full...
When I haven't eaten anything at all!

I wondered if I could get it out!
LIke my cat Harry gets a furball out.
I asked Grandpa about my plan...
He said, "IT MIGHT WORK, without a doubt!"

I coughed and I coughed!
My family and friends ran to me!
When the giant lint ball flew out of my mouth...
I hope it was the most disgusting thing I'll ever see!

HOLIDAY

It's been a long, long time
Since we've been away.
A long, long time
Since we've had a holiday!

So, when I started off to school
And something led me astray...
I was surprised when I discovered
Inside me was a holiday!

Next thing I knew I was making sand castles...
On a sunny, tropical beach.
We were sitting right near the ocean...
Where the dolphins seemed within reach.

Then a man in a straw hat...
Said he'd teach me how to surf.
I tried but I kept tumbling into the waves...
And that night we ate Surf & Turf!

Next thing I knew school was over!
I was on my way back home with glee!
Feeling refreshed thanks to...
The holiday inside of me!

LLAMA

I met a llama at the zoo...
And now she lives inside of me.
I can't get a single minute to myself...
Because she keeps following me!

"*Ah!*" I cry, as I try to escape from her...
My brother laughs while I look grim.
But he doesn't think it is so funny when...
The llama starts following and spitting at him!

LEMON MERINGUE PIE

I don't like lemons at all!
And they don't like me.
Then how come a Lemon Meringue Pie...
Moved inside of me?

It seems like a very bad joke...
If you ask me...
When something I do not like...
Moves inside of me!

If it were a Chocolate Cake...
Now that would sure be grand!
I'd slice it into portions...
And eat them up with my hands!

Or if it were Carrot Cake...
Or Cheesecake would be even better!
Instead of eating a Lemon Meringue Pie
I'd prefer to eat my sweater!

AUTUMN

Summer ended very fast!
And autumn flew inside of me.
Back to school, hayrides, and Halloween...
Spectacular colours on every tree!

Autumn flies by faster than...
Any other season I see.
Which is why I appreciate it more...
When Autumn turns Wintery.

BOON

I was sitting under a tree reading a book...
When a boon flew inside of me.
It introduced itself...
I didn't know what a boon was you see.

The boon said it had been looking for me...
To make one of my dreams come true.
It said it could be a dream or a wish...
Either one would do.

The wind rustled in the tree above me
A single leaf floated into my hand.
I placed it between the pages of my book...
Then I decided to stand.

I knew the boon inside of me
Was waiting for a reply.
But I couldn't think of a wish or a dream to request...
Now we're friends the boon and I!

RAM

A ram is a male sheep.
A female sheep is a ewe.
It is easier to count sheep at night...
When one is living inside of you.

SCOOTER

I saw a scooter riding by...
Its driver was a duck you see.
Next thing I knew the scooter...
Ducked inside of me!

The scooter hummed. The duck quacked...
Both are for sale or for free...
Please reply if you know how...
To get them out of me!

WRITE OR DRAW HERE...

WRITE OR DRAW
ABOUT YOUR HOLIDAY

ALSO BY CATHY MCGOUGH

POETRY SERIES:

There's a Chimpanzee Inside of Me!
There's a Jumping Bean Inside of Me!
There's a Reindeer Inside of Me!
There's a Hero inside of Me!
There's a Panda inside of Me!
There's a Mock Turtle inside of Me!
There's a Spaceship inside of Me!

JUMP SERIES:

Jump Like a Caribou!
Jump Like a Kangaroo!
Jump at the Zoo!
Jump and Say P.U.!
Jump and Say Boo!
Jump and Say Valentine's Day Is
For Kids Too!
Jump and Look For a Clue!
Jump and Say Happy Birthday to You!
Jump For Everything Blue!
Jump, Hop and Say Happy Easter To You!
Jump and Say Cock-A-Doodle-Do!
Jump and Sing Da-Do-Do-Do!
Jump and Ask Who? Who?
Jump and Squawk Like a Cockatoo!
Jump and Ask Is It You or Ewe?
Jump and Say There's an Ewww in My Stew!
Jump and Say Merry Christmas To You!
Jump and Cheer Happy New Year!
Jump and Say There's a Moo-Moo in a Tutu!
Jump and Say There's a Hare in My Hair!
Jump and Say My Aunt Ate An Ant!
Jump and Say There's An Aardvark
In The Amusement Park!
Jump and Roar For The Dinosaurs!
Jump and Buzz Like A Bee!
Jump and Flutter Like A Butterfly!
Jump and Pop Like Popcorn!
Jump and Ribbit Like A Frog!
Jump and Snore Like A Koala!

Jump and Snuffle Like A Platypus!
Jump and Grunt Like A Groundhog!
Jump and Say Hello!
Jump and Say Friend!
Jump and Say Peace!
Jump and Say Sky!
Jump and Say Merry Christmas!
Jump and Say Happy New Year!
Jump and Say Fun!
Jump and Say Family!
Jump and Say Jump!

CLAP FOR SERIES:

Clap for 1!
Clap for 2!
Clap for 3!
Clap for 4!
Clap for 5!
Clap for 6!
Clap for 7!
Clap for 8!
Clap for 9!
Clap for 10!

The Cat Who Said Hello
The Three Boulders
Billy Shakespeare
Billie Shakespeare
Learn To Draw With Symmetry
ABC More Learn to Draw With Symmetry

Non-Fiction
103 Fundraising Ideas For Parent Volunteers With Schools and Teams